CROCODILES, PYRAMIDS AND KINGS

Herodotus in Egypt

Grant Bage

Crosslinks

Series Editors
Grant Bage
Deborah Ramsbotham

First published in 2002
by Anglia Young Books

Anglia Young Books is an imprint of
Mill Publishing Ltd
PO Box 120
Bangor
County Down
BT19 7BX

Illustrations by Robin Lawrie
Design by Angela Ashton

British Library Cataloguing-in-Publication Data

A catalogue record for this book is available from the British Library

ISBN 1 871173 80 9

Printed in Great Britain by Ashford Colour Press, Gosport, Hampshire

CONTENTS PAGE

WHO IS HERODOTUS?

Herodotus may sound like a strange name from an old book, but behind every name is a person. In these pages that person is me, Herodotus. I lived long ago in Ancient Greece and I wrote the first set of information books the world has ever known. For years my slaves and I scratched patiently, with writing sticks and black ink, on to long rolls of yellow papyrus. We marked each roll carefully with letters and words, building up reports, explanations and discussions. You can find all of these in my books. I will share some with you and I will make you a promise. They will not be dull. My 'information' is like most people's 'stories', full of colourful characters and interesting facts.

I am proud of my writing, if you will forgive a

little boast from a man who lived two and a half thousand years ago. In those days we spoke and we listened more than we read and wrote: writing was only just catching on, even in schools. Not that most people *read* my writing, on paper: that would have put me out of a job. Anyway, printing was not invented for another two thousand years, so copying books was difficult. No, what I wrote, I read aloud to an audience. They would sit on benches or on the grass under the olive trees, with figs to chew on and wine to drink; then I would start my stories.

People liked to hear what was written, spoken by the person who wrote it: then they could stop at different points and ask things. Writing also helped to remind me what was important: I had so much to remember that, without writing, I might forget the facts or muddle things up. I travelled for most of my long life and, over time, different bits of my writing grew into the books you now call the 'histories'. In Ancient Greek 'history' meant 'enquiry'. That is what I did: I enquired. Some people called me 'nosy' but I just loved finding things out. I travelled to Asia, to Africa and through much of Europe. I enquired about the world's rivers, mountains, peoples, gods, battles, heroes and stories – there is so much to know! Then, when I had found out all about something, I wrote down as much as I could remember.

In this book I must choose just a few tales to tell you from the thousands I know. I have travelled the world on foot, on horseback, in a carriage and by boat. I have tramped dusty roads, in beating sun and driving rain, from north to south to east and back. I have even heard tell of a strange land far away in the west, home of glittering tin and gleaming gold. 'Britain' I think they call it, a place full of barbarians and of no importance. So let me tell you about another country, one older even than Greek cities like Athens or Sparta. This is a land of mystery and might, a wonder of the world. I was lucky enough to visit it often. I doubt you will have heard of it, barbarians as you are, but to many of us Greeks it was the home of all knowledge: its name is Egypt.

1
SEEING IS BELIEVING

How do I know about Egypt? I did what any
intelligent person does when they want to find
things out. I travelled and looked closely at the
people: the jobs they were doing in their fields,
houses and towns, the clothes they wore, the foods
they ate, the gods they worshipped. I studied the
lands they lived in: was the weather hotter or
colder than in Greece? Was the country wet as a
flood or dry as a bone? Were there mountains and
rivers and forests? I listened carefully to what
people told me as they showed me around this
village or that temple. Then I made friends with
lawyers, merchants, priests and queens. In jobs
like these you must know the stories of your

people and have a sharp memory; you might even speak Greek too. After listening to their stories and asking lots of questions, I wrote things down. That is why my books are still being read two and a half thousand years later. If I had not written these things down, who would remember them now?

"Get back to the subject in hand, Herodotus."

That is what my old teacher used to tell me when I was chatting in class. Now what *was* the subject? Oh yes, Egypt, that wonderful country. If you want to discover Egypt for yourself, you should do as I did and float along the Nile. The Nile is the cool, wide river without which nothing could live. The sun beats down upon Egypt and only a few miles from the river all is hot sand and dry rock. But by the river it is wet and it is heaven. The fields are green, the soil is damp and the river is full of fish, birds and crocodiles – but that is another story that I will tell you later! Let me start by recounting some special events that I have seen with my own eyes: what happens on holy days – or 'holidays' as you call them.

The Egyptians taught us Greeks which gods to worship and how to run festivals full of fun and even fear. The largest festival is for the hunter goddess and this is what happens. Barges sail down the River Nile, crammed with people. Some of the men play tunes on flutes and some of the women beat a rhythm on small wooden instruments, while the others sing and clap their hands. When the barges pass through a town, they sail close to the shore and the noise of the dancing and singing grows even louder. Sometimes women even dance with their skirts over their heads! So it goes on, until the barges reach Bubastis, a fine city at the mouth of the Nile about forty kilometres from the sea. Here the people dance through the streets and drink lots of wine. People who have been there tell me that hundreds of thousands of people take part, and that is not even counting the children.

Another city leads the festival of the lamps. Sacred cows are paraded through the streets and worshipped, and bulls and sheep are sacrificed. Then as night falls, the lighting of the lamps begins. Each house has first one lamp flickering in the dusk, then another and another. The lamps are flat, clay dishes, filled to the brim with oil and salt. A wick floats in the oil and it can burn all night. What a sight to see – thousands of tiny flames flaring in the dark towns and villages of Egypt.

There are many festivals but let me tell you about just one more. This strange event happens in another town, at the temple of the god of war. As the sun sets, the priests stop their ordinary work of chanting or saying prayers. They bless themselves and solemnly choose a wooden stick from a pile that has been prepared. These sticks are long and thick – 'clubs' we call them – and they are frightening weapons. The priests file out to the temple entrance and line up, grim looks on their faces. Opposite them is another and greater crowd, of perhaps a thousand men. Each man in this crowd has a promise or a question for the god of war: these men are about to worship him.

You may have guessed what is about to happen, but let me explain anyway. All temples have statues, but this statue is different: it *moves*. Before the day of the festival, a few priests carefully place the statue in a gold-plated box, called a 'shrine'. Then they carry it far away. On the night of the festival they wheel the statue back on a cart, dragging it with ropes towards the temple. The men in the crowd outside join forces with these few priests, to carry the statue of the

god back into the temple. First though, they have to break through the long line of priests who were left behind. These priests are armed with wooden clubs, the ones I told you about earlier. The fighting is fierce and, please believe me, the blood and the bruises are real. The priests swing their wooden clubs and crash them down, as the men battle with their fists and feet to carry the statue back into the temple.

The Egyptians I spoke to claimed that nobody had ever been killed during this festival, but I did not believe them. How could such fights happen without a death or two?

2
REPORTING ON EGYPT

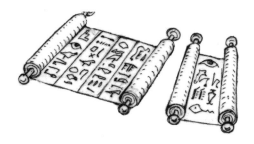

I have recounted events I saw for myself in Egypt and stories of happenings that people told me about. Now I shall give a fuller report, of the country as a whole. To start with, you cannot understand Egypt unless you know that it is a very old place. Egypt was ancient even two and a half thousand years ago when I was child, as fresh and lively as you. Like many Greek children I was fascinated by tales of 'Ancient Egypt', tales told to us by slaves and travellers. There were stories of stone pyramids as tall as mountains, built for kings and queens; of bodies lying in them, thousands of years after their deaths but still not rotten. People said there were priests who could see into the future, scaly monsters who lived in rivers, tombs of gold, silver and precious stones.

I will not tell you all of those stories. Instead, I will report on what I know from experience, or believe to be true. That is what a report does: it lists important things you need to know and sometimes it explains them. The Egyptians were the wisest people then on earth because they made a habit of writing things down. If something unusual or interesting happened, or if somebody owed some money, a record was made. A scribe might have written a list on papyrus. (Scribes were people who wrote things down for priests or kings.) The Egyptians also made carvings on stone, paintings on walls and marks in clay. They used all these different ways of writing to produce lists, reports and stories. This is why they knew more than most people about history. But they were not just interested in the past – they also wrote about how healthy they felt, in the present.

In Egypt you could pay a doctor to tell you about each part of your body. The doctor's job was to know all about your eyes, your teeth, or your particular illness. Many of the Egyptians I met ate no food for three days in every month and they took medicines to make them go to the toilet. This is because they believed that illnesses came from the food they ate, so people wanted to clear out their stomachs. Perhaps it was because of this medicine, or maybe it was the weather, or the doctors, but Egypt seemed the healthiest place I ever visited. Or perhaps it was the Egyptians' diet. They ate loaves of bread made from wheat and drank wine made from barley – they did not grow grapes. Fish was a favourite food, mostly caught using nets or lines in the River Nile, or even the sea. Some fish were roasted in a clay oven or boiled in a pot. Other fish were hung out to dry in the sun or salted so that they could be eaten later. Birds were eaten too: small birds that lived in the trees and bigger ones such as ducks, caught by the river.

And here is a strange thing to report, something that rich people did at parties. When the meal was finished and the guests' stomachs were full, a servant took round a special model. It was like a wooden doll but it showed a dead person lying in a coffin. The body was carefully carved, painted to seem just like the real thing. It was quite large too – between fifty and a hundred centimetres long. The model was shown to each of the guests in turn. They were told: "Look down at this body as you eat, drink and enjoy yourself: for this will be you, when you are dead." It seems a strange thing to do at a party but in the ancient world, even if you tried to stay healthy, death was always close. Death could visit a child, a priest or a queen at any time, without warning. Remember that ...

Perhaps that is why the Egyptians were so interested in death, as well as health. For example when a rich man died, the dead body was laid out flat in his house. To begin the funeral, the women of the house smeared wet mud all over their heads and filed outside, their faces and cheeks streaked with mud. Waiting for them were other members of the family, men and women, their clothes tightly tied with special funeral-belts. The whole crowd walked around the village, sometimes beating themselves and wailing to show their sorrow. When they got back to the house the dead body was taken away and 'mummified'. I discovered great secrets about this magical act of 'mummification', secrets I may tell you later.

That is enough about death. Let me now

report on birth. You already know that the Egyptians recorded things in writing, especially important or unusual events. When a baby was born, priests could read these records and use them to see into the baby's future. In Egypt, every day and each of their twelve months had a different god. The baby's family visited the temple of the god or goddess of the baby's birth month. The mother reported the day and the place of the birth, and any strange things that were happening at the time. The priest or priestess then read or remembered things about that day or place from other babies, born years before. Then the priest looked at the parents and at the baby. All this knowledge was stirred together in the priest's mind and used to predict the baby's future. This 'future' was then told to the parents: perhaps a poor life and an early death, maybe fame and riches. Finally, the parents offered a gift to the temple and to the priest, before trudging back home. Did it work? Could these priests really see into the future? I am not sure: go and ask your own god ...

There is so much to report about Egypt that I could go on for ever. That is what books are for.

Books can go on for ever, if somebody reads them.
Here am I talking to you, but I have been dead for
over two thousand years. Books help you learn
from the past and from people older than you.
This is the last thing I shall report. In Egypt,
young people were polite to their elders. If a young
Egyptian met an old person in the street, he would
step to one side and let them pass. If an old man
or woman came into a room, the young men and
women stood up from their seats. This was called
'good manners' – perhaps it still is. So next time
you are told off for having 'bad manners',
remember that people have always had to learn to
be polite and kind. Remember, too, that it was old
Herodotus who reported from Ancient Egypt on
fortune-telling, funerals, death, health and
writing. But now I will move on to explain some
more mysteries about Greece, about Egypt and
about life.

3
EXPLAINING EGYPT

I love words, as you can probably tell. One reason I started writing was because I wanted other people to love words too. However, words are only one way of explaining the world. Think about maths, for example. A number is like a word, because you can say it and write it down. But numbers are *not* like words because they can be multiplied or subtracted to make completely different numbers. In Greece we came to love numbers and we became very clever at maths. To be honest, Pythagoras was the cleverest, much cleverer than me. He taught us how the number 10 was really a triangle, whichever way you looked at it, and lots more besides.

Guess what, though (and I am sure you can)! I thought — and so did many of my friends — that we Greeks learnt our maths from Egypt. When I asked Egyptian priests about their old kings and queens, they read to me from a list of three hundred and thirty names. One name was that of a king who lived a thousand years before my visit and long before Pythagoras. Maths really mattered to him. He used numbers to divide up his own land. Let me explain. Some of his towns were in hot and dusty lands, far from the cool River Nile. He wanted to get water to these dry towns and the only way was to dig dykes. (A dyke is a deep ditch through which water can flow.) If Egypt was to be criss-crossed with dykes, it would take a lot of working out. Farmers would argue if one dyke was close to them and another far away, for it would make some farmers' work easy and others' very hard. The problem had to be solved and the king used maths to do it. He divided his land into square fields of equal size and then asked all the farmers to pay taxes equal to the amount of land they owned. This king also built towering temples and soaring statues, every one measured in just the right way. This was how we Greeks came to know so much about numbers and shapes – we learnt our maths from the Egyptians.

The Egyptians borrowed things from the Greeks too. Some of them were there in my day and still are. Take the crocodile, for instance. This creature lives in the Nile; I shall say more about it shortly. The word 'crocodile' comes from our Greek words meaning 'stone' and 'lizard'. The lizards in Greece are small creatures that live on walls and in fields, but the crocodiles of Egypt are enormous beasts up to seven metres long. They swim in rivers and eat animals, people and each other, tearing flesh with their strong claws, grinding it lifeless between two great sets of teeth. People told me that crocodiles could see a long way on land but were blind under water. I could not be certain of this, but there is one thing I can tell you. Crocodiles eat just about anything apart from one type of bird called a sandpiper. This bird not only hops around crocodiles without getting eaten, it even gets inside their mouths!

The explanation I gave for this odd event is simple and I think it is still true two and a half thousand years later. Crocodiles live under water for much of their life. In the water live small creatures that look and wriggle like worms. They are called leeches and they live by sucking blood. Crocodiles have large mouths with many teeth so the leeches can swim in. Soon they find the flesh of the crocodile's mouth just above its teeth and bite hard, sucking blood. Crocodiles do not like this but there is little they can do. Their legs are too short and their claws too sharp to get the leeches out without injuring themselves. That is where the bird comes in – or, should I say, flies in? On hot days, crocodiles like to lie with their mouths wide open because it helps keep them cool. The sharp-eyed birds spot the leeches wriggling inside the crocodile's mouth and, with a flap and a glide, in they fly to peck up the leeches with their long beaks. You might think that the crocodile would snap its jaws shut and gobble up the bird, but they do not. Do they know that the bird is helping them? Or maybe it is because they only lie with their mouths open when they have a full stomach, so they are not hungry anyway? Whatever the explanation, the crocodile was just one more of Egypt's wonders. It still is, I believe.

I cannot finish there. Let me tell you one last thing about how clever the Egyptians were. In

Egypt, hunters had many crafty ways of catching crocodiles but I shall explain just one. Crocodiles eat meat, as I have told you before, and one of their favourites is pig meat. The hunters knew this and they used pigs to set traps. One hunter would take a large pork chop and fasten it on to a hook. The hook was on a long line that was floated out into the middle of the river, close to the crocodiles. Then the hunter's friend, safe on the riverbank, would beat a live pig with a stick. The squeals of the pig told the crocodile that lunch was in the river and off it swam to find it. On the way, it smelt the pork chop and swallowed it down, not knowing the meat had a hook and line inside. At that moment, the hunters started pulling the line. Soon the crocodile was thrashing about in the water, trying to escape but it could not. When it was tired out, the hunters pulled the crocodile on to dry land. It was still dangerous until one final trick had been played. As the crocodile lay there panting, one of the hunters would creep up from behind and plaster its eyes with mud. The crocodile was blinded and could not see the hunters approaching silently, their spears sharpened for the kill ...

Now let me ask you – no, I will *instruct* you – never go near a river with crocodiles. Egyptian mothers and fathers never tired of telling their children this and they pointed out the pools where crocodiles might lurk. This did not stop several children every year being eaten by these scaly monsters. It is sad that children do not always follow orders, but that reminds me of a story I have wanted to tell again for several thousand years. If you want to hear it, turn to the next chapter. Now, that is an instruction …

4
NOW, MY SON, FOLLOW THESE INSTRUCTIONS

Have you ever noticed how some adults just love to be clever? I like clever people as long as they listen to *my* ideas, as well as telling me *their* ideas. But there are some adults – and children – who use cleverness in a different way. They want you to believe they are clever so that they can boss you around. Once they can boss *you* around, they start on everybody else. In the cities of Ancient Greece, this was a good way to start an argument: one person just telling others what to do, without listening to what the people wanted. We called these men 'tyrants' and I tried never to obey them.

Instructions should be words that help you to

think for yourself and understand what to do. It does not always work like that, as you will see in this story. The story is about a man who refused to follow somebody else's instructions and gained great riches by giving his own. Now I think about it, the story is full of instructions. So let me begin, while you listen ... and that is an order.

About eight hundred years before I was born, in the rich and powerful country of Egypt, there ruled a rich and powerful king. His name was Rhampsinitus and he had so much silver that he did not know what to do with it. He tried spending it on stone statues fifteen metres high. He tried spending it on clothes to make *him* look fifteen metres high. He tried spending it on chariots and swords and soldiers, and all the other things kings like to make themselves look clever. It did not work. He did not look clever and he had lots of silver left. So the king gave orders to build a huge stone store for his treasure.

"Find me the cleverest builder in the land, to design a treasury. Tell him to build it in stone and to make sure it is safe from thieves. And he must build it in double quick time," the king snapped.

Giving orders and getting them followed are

two different things. The king liked the treasury that the royal builder built, but the builder did not like the king. (Nobody else did either.) Now the builder had a secret. On his deathbed, he passed it on to his two sons, making them swear to keep the secret.

The secret was this. The builder had been planning the roof, measuring the walls, giving orders to the stonemasons, organising the slaves and being polite to the king: but he had already decided to make one stone just a little bit special. This would be his stone, not the king's. It was hidden away around a bend, down a passage, in the dark, so that no one would notice it. It was cut by the builder's own hand to look like every other stone. But, as he whispered to his sons as he lay dying, this stone was different. This stone would move if they pushed it in the right place, pulled it the right way, twisted it at the right angle and slid the slab down.

"Remember my instructions, to the letter," gasped the old man, "and this family will be rich for ever."

So it was that the builder died and the sons … well, they just followed their instructions. They walked past the palace and, when no one was looking, they dived into the bushes to find their father's special stone. Remembering what their father had said, they pushed, pulled, twisted and slid the stone and climbed inside the treasury. Soon their pockets were filled with silver.

The trouble with luck is that it makes some people greedy. Once, twice, three times the brothers visited the treasury and all went well. When they went back a fourth time though, things turned out differently. The first brother squirmed through the gap and slid his hand greedily into the money jar. But inside the jar was a trap that snapped shut on his hand. Worse still, a snake slithered out and bit his hand. He knew he would be dead within a minute. This helped him to think even more quickly than usual.

"Aaagh!" he screamed to his brother, who was just scrambling out of the tunnel. "I am trapped and bitten and doomed. I shall be dead in a minute, once the snake poison works. Listen carefully and do what I say. Cut off my head when I am dead and carry it away, so that our secret stays safe." Then he gurgled, turned blue and died.

Of course the second brother was in a panic

but what could he do? He filled his pockets with silver from another jar, chopped off his dead brother's head and placed it in a sack. Then he climbed back through the hole in the wall and carefully replaced the stone.

When the king visited his silver the next morning, you can imagine his astonishment. A headless body lay in the trap and more silver was missing but there was no sign of how the two thieves had come in – or of how one thief had got out. The king knew he would have to be as clever as a thief to catch the survivor.

"Hang that headless body in chains, high from my palace walls," he ordered, with a snarl. Then secretly he instructed a spy to hide by the body and watch carefully for any person stopping and crying at the dreadful sight. Such a person must be a relative and could lead him back to the thief that had got away.

What was the surviving brother to do? His mother wept all day at the thought of his dead brother's headless body, hanging in chains.

"Go and get that body back," she screamed. That was one order the brother had to obey, but how?

You will trust him, I am sure, to come up with a plan, since he came from such a clever family. And that is why, the very next day, the brother was to be seen leading the family donkey, piled high with flagons of wine, past the spot where the body was hanging. As the brother and his donkey reached the guards, he pulled a hidden string and the flagons rolled off the donkey's back, as if by accident. One broke on the stones and the others rolled down the road. The donkey brayed in alarm and the brother roared with false anger as the soldiers chased the tumbling flagons. As they trundled them back, he thanked the soldiers kindly and opened a flagon: would they share some wine with him?

You can guess the rest. The soldiers drank one mug of wine, then another and then a few more. The brother laughed and joked with them but his mug was filled with water. In the shake of a donkey's tail, the flies were buzzing lazily around the snoring soldiers, drunk in the warmth of an Egyptian dusk. Quick as a thief (for indeed he was a thief), the brother took down his brother's body and rode off into the night.

He had followed his father's instructions. He

had followed his brother's instructions. He had followed his mother's instructions too. Now he had learnt that he must think for himself. It was time for a deep sleep and a quiet life!

5
MAKING OUR MINDS UP

So far I have recounted, reported, explained, and told a story to make you think about instructions. But Egypt was also full of mysteries, things that people could not understand or agree about however long they talked. Let you and I discuss some of these mysteries and then you can make up your own mind.

For instance, were the Egyptians the first people on earth? This sort of question is still good for an argument. I have noticed the same sort of thing with children, when they run outside after school. They are soon squabbling about whose turn it is to swing on the rope hanging from the olive tree, or to swim in the pool by the stream. "I was here first," somebody always says. "No, I was," somebody else shouts, louder.

Grown-ups say things like that too, especially when they are arguing. The Egyptians thought a lot about the question 'Who were the first people on earth?' They just could not agree on an answer. It seems an odd thing to argue about, but it was as important to them as 'which team came first', or 'choosing your best friend'. And it leads me on to another story that I discussed with priests, when I visited Ancient Egypt. This story settled the old, old argument.

Not long before my visit, a man named Psammetichus became king of Egypt. He had listened to endless discussions about 'Who were the first people on earth?' and he was sick of them. To answer the question once and for all he did an *experiment*, one that you might think was cruel.

He found an ordinary mother who had just given birth to twins and he took the babies away from her. No discussion, no argument, he just did it: kings were like that in those days. Then he gave the babies to a shepherd who lived far away from the babies' family and far from any town. The king gave strict instructions that nobody should say a single word to the two babies. They were to be kept alone in a hut and every so often the shepherd was to bring in goats and let the babies suck their milk. It sounds like cruel madness but remember that the king was trying to find something out. Can you see what he was up to?

Let me tell you. The babies grew quickly, having as much fresh goat's milk as they could drink. They started to wave their hands and legs, as babies do, and later to sit up and crawl. No human being was allowed to speak to them, though the babies cooed and gurgled and babbled to themselves. The shepherd kept a close eye on the growing infants, partly to protect them but also because the king had given orders. The king was waiting for a special day and he did not want to miss it.

That day came when the children were about two years old. The shepherd opened the door of the hut as usual, to let in the goats. This time the children did not sit and wait for the goat's milk. Instead they ran towards the shepherd with their arms stretched out, mouthing the first word he had ever heard them speak. "*Becos, becos,*" they said. "*Becos, becos,*" they begged. What did *becos* mean?

The shepherd hurried to tell the king. The king ordered the children to be brought to him, so he could hear them speak for himself. *"Becos, becos,"* the children crooned to the king, as they had done to the shepherd. So the king ordered the scholars and priests, those people who could read and write, to enquire what the word might mean.

And that is how the argument about 'Who were the first people on earth?' was settled. *Becos* meant 'bread', but it was not a word from Egypt. It was a word from the Phrygians, a Greek people who lived many hundreds of miles from Egypt and quite near where I, Herodotus, lived. The king's experiment had shown that the Egyptians could not have been the first people on earth, and that the Greeks probably were.

I heard some daft versions of this story in Greece, including one in which the children were brought up by women who had had their tongues cut out. Stories are like that – there is never just one way of telling them. This is true of 'facts' as well: there is always something to think about and discuss. Take the River Nile, in Egypt. Now you might know something about this river already. For instance, it was a well-known fact in my day

that the Nile flooded every summer and that this was good for Egypt, not bad. Inch by inch the river crept up until the muddy water swirled round the top of the banks. The water lapped higher and higher until it swilled over the banks and beyond, flowing through ditches and dykes, flooding the special fields that the farmers had made. Without this water, Egypt would have starved: there would have been too many people to feed from the dry and dusty land. So the floods fed the people of Egypt, but why did these floods happen in the first place? And even stranger, why did the Nile flood in summer when it was driest and not in winter when there was more rain?

Clever Greeks (or rather Greeks who liked to *think* they were clever) were always discussing *why* the River Nile flooded each summer. There were four explanations. The hard part for me was deciding which one was best, and why. Let me explain, then you can discuss it and make up your own minds.

The first explanation was from people who said that the Nile flowed from an ocean and that a stream from the ocean somehow flowed round the world. "Look around you," these people said.

"However big a country is, sooner or later it always comes up against water. Most of the earth is water – that water must flow from an ocean, and so must the Nile." But where was that ocean? And why was the Nile freshwater, not saltwater?

The second lot of people thought differently, believing the flooding was more to do with wind than water. "Feel the north wind blowing in summer," they said. "It is pushing the water from the Nile south, back down the river. That is why it floods." They seemed to forget that the Nile always flooded but the winds did not always blow.

The third explanation was even stranger. Some people believed that the Nile flooded because snow melted, somewhere far off in the mountains. "Look at the rivers in Greece," they said. "When the snow melts in spring they flow and flood like crazy. Why should the Nile be any different?" They seemed to forget that the Nile flowed from far away in the south and only flooded as it got to the north. Yet everybody knew, then as now, that the south of a country is always hotter than the north. So how could there be snow and frost in the middle of Africa, from where the River Nile appeared to come?

The fourth group of people was the cleverest. In the interests of a fair discussion, I suppose I should admit that 'they' are really 'me', Herodotus. I had my own ideas about why the Nile floods. "Look at the bad winter storms to the west of Egypt," I said to my listeners. "They knock the sun off course. The sun hovers over those western lands and dries them up, drawing all the moisture into itself." People often nodded in agreement at this point, though some looked a bit puzzled. "Then in summer when the storms have finished," I would continue, "the sun goes back to its normal place over Egypt. It drops all the water back on to the land. That is why the River Nile floods in summer."

It seems obvious to me that this was by far the best explanation. If you do not believe me, try discussing it among yourselves or looking it up in a book. Rumour has it, though, that for some reason in your times the Nile has stopped flooding. I cannot imagine such a thing: it could never have happened in my day.

6
SO, YOU THINK YOU ARE HAPPY? LET ME PERSUADE YOU OTHERWISE

You can do good things with words and bad things too. Words can persuade people to think or act in ways they might not want to. Words can turn people into heroes or villains. Words can make you happy, or miserable. Let me finish this book with some words of persuasion and wisdom, wrapped up in a story.

The story is about a teacher called Solon and a king called Croesus. Solon was so wise that he was asked to write a new set of laws for the great Greek city of Athens. He agreed, but only if the citizens of Athens promised to try out the new laws for ten years without changing any of them. So when his laws were written, Solon left Athens and travelled the world.

That is why one day he arrived in a country ruled by King Croesus. The king was glad to entertain such a famous and clever man. He was looking forward to showing off in front of him. So to make Solon welcome, the king sent him on a tour of all the royal palaces and treasuries. The king wanted to impress the clever Athenian and persuade him that he, King Croesus, was the greatest of men.

"Solon," said the king, after Solon had returned from this tour, "you have seen how rich and beautiful my land is, with its fine palaces and bulging treasuries, its stone temples and flowering fields. Now I must ask you a question: who is the happiest man you have ever heard of?"

This was a trick question, as you have probably guessed. The king wanted Solon to say, "Why you of course, great king." But Solon was too clever for that. He wanted to persuade the king to be humble and wise, in case the gods were watching his false pride and decided to cut him down to size. He thought for a few moments about his answer and then turned to the king and said:

"Well, a man in Athens called Tellus was the happiest man I ever knew. He had fine children, and all these children had children of their own. His business made him rich and his city was prospering. Then he was killed in battle, but even that was good, for he died a hero. His friends loved him so much that they held a public funeral for him, at exactly the spot where he was killed. That is what I call happiness: people thinking well of you when you are gone."

The king smiled but he was not happy. How dare this clever-clogs visitor try to persuade everybody that King Croesus was not the happiest man alive? "Very good, my dear Solon," the king replied in an oily voice, "who is the second happiest man you have ever seen?" Surely, the king thought, it must be him.

"Actually there were two of them," said Solon, "and they were brothers. They were strong and earned good money. They did well at the games and in athletic contests. Then one day there was a special festival for the goddess Hera. The boys' mother wanted to be driven to the temple in her ox-cart, but the oxen were late back from the fields. So the boys got into the oxen's harness and dragged their mother to the temple – six miles in all. All the men marvelled at their strength and the women paid the mother compliments, at having such thoughtful sons."

"So happiness is being an ox, is it?" smirked the king.

"Oh no," replied Solon. "The truly happy thing was that the young men were so tired that they lay down in the temple and went to sleep. They never woke up. The goddess Hera was so impressed by what she had seen, that she kept the boys for herself. The mother was upset, of course, but knew that the goddess had blessed her sons; and the people of the town made statues of the boys that still stand to this day."

By this time, the king was mad with jealousy. "How can these common people be thought of as happier than me? They are all dead for a start," he fumed. So Solon tried one last time to persuade King Croesus to change his mind about what might make a man happy.

"Listen, my good king," he sighed, patiently. "If you live to be seventy years old, that is twenty

six thousand, two hundred and fifty days or so (depending on whether you use the Greek calendar or the Egyptian one). But not one of those days is the same as another. Life is full of chance and my point is this: until you reach the end of your life, how can you say it is happy? Things can change at any moment. You are very rich and you have soldiers and servants. But a poor person can have as much luck as a rich one. A poor person works hard in the fields and is more likely to have a strong and healthy body, freedom from worries, fine children and good looks. Listen to my words carefully, King Croesus. Keep the word 'happy' hidden away, out of sight. For until you reach the end of your life you can never call yourself 'happy': you can only call yourself 'lucky'."

King Croesus was not persuaded. Nor was he happy to be told foolish words by a wise man, so he sent Solon packing to another country. As you may have guessed, that was the beginning of the end for the king. We Greeks had words for what happened to Croesus: the first was *hubris*. *Hubris* meant arrogance and pride – but it was false pride, for the person would soon fall. The second word was *nemesis*. This described what happened afterwards, when the gods and goddesses brought that person to their knees. Be persuaded, my dear listeners, for shortly after scorning Solon, Croesus's son was killed in a hunting accident, his army was defeated, his city burnt and to this day nobody knows what happened to him. Croesus became famous, but for the wrong reason. He became famous because he could not be persuaded by Solon, one of the wisest of men, of what it took for a person to be happy.

Now, have I persuaded *you*?

THE LIFE OF HERODOTUS

Herodotus wrote the world's first information books and he has been called 'the father of history', but we don't know much about him. We know he was from a well-known Greek family and that he was born in 484 BC in a small town called Halicarnassus on what is now the west coast of Turkey. It was on the frontier between two powers – the Greeks and the Persians – and, when Herodotus was young, they were at war.

When Herodotus was much older, he wrote his 'Histories', a series of nine books to describe and explain the war with Persia. However, Herodotus was also trying to write a 'world history' in a way that had never been done before. Until then, Greek poets like Homer had based their writing about the past on myths, gods and heroes. Herodotus worked differently. He travelled the world, *enquiring* – seeking information from eyewitnesses, written records, local legends, site visits and observations. He then wrote down his enquiries, *recording* events from recent life as well as from the more distant past, based upon different sources of evidence. He was working rather like a journalist or historian might do today.

Herodotus became the first great European writer of what we call 'factual' or 'non-fiction' writing. However, he also told stories to get his facts across, reporting on interesting people and exciting events. Herodotus was a great storyteller, but his stories are 'real'. He died sometime between 425 and 420 BC.